YOUR KNOWLEDGE HA

- We will publish your bachelor's and master's thesis, essays and papers

- Your own eBook and book - sold worldwide in all relevant shops

- Earn money with each sale

Upload your text at www.GRIN.com and publish for free

Bibliographic information published by the German National Library:

The German National Library lists this publication in the National Bibliography; detailed bibliographic data are available on the Internet at http://dnb.dnb.de .

Imprint:

Copyright © 2016 GRIN Verlag, Open Publishing GmbH
Print and binding: Books on Demand GmbH, Norderstedt Germany
ISBN: 9783668335592

This book at GRIN:

http://www.grin.com/en/e-book/343195/construction-of-a-master-data-management-strategy-methodologies-and-tools

Florette Chamga

Construction of a master data management strategy. Methodologies and tools

GRIN Publishing

GRIN - Your knowledge has value

Since its foundation in 1998, GRIN has specialized in publishing academic texts by students, college teachers and other academics as e-book and printed book. The website www.grin.com is an ideal platform for presenting term papers, final papers, scientific essays, dissertations and specialist books.

Visit us on the internet:

http://www.grin.com/

http://www.facebook.com/grincom

http://www.twitter.com/grin_com

Construcion of a master data management strategy: methodologies and tools

Content

Seminar thesis

Construction of a master data management strategy: methodologies and tools

Florette Chamga T.

Heilbronn University, Faculty of Information systems

03.07.2016

Abstract

In a world governed by mobile internet and characterized by an increasing number of active customers on the way, companies have to face the difficulty of implementing an adequate strategy for proper master data management. The drastic increase in active mobile connection of both companies and customers leads to rapid master data growth and therefore points out the necessity of implementing a management strategy. The construction of a master data management strategy implies the interaction of different tools and methodologies. Starting with an overview of existing literature and limiting itself within the given scope, the present review then handles the interaction proper. This constitutes the essential component of this work

Keywords: master data management(MDM), master data management strategy, master data management solution, "Stammdatenpflege"

1 Introduction

1.1 Problem statement

Check a friend's address on google map or consult incoming mails using a smartphone is though "normal" task, but also implies and exponential increase of information exchange. Most software systems have lists of data, master data, which is shared and used by several of the applications that make up the system and will also be subjected to an exponential expansion. Furthermore, a company might grow through merger and this logically implies there will be a need to merge all available data which can be a cumbersome task. It would therefore be judicious to think of a strategy to facilitate all this management stuff and thus increase productivity.

1.2 Research question

Just like going to war requires having the necessary weapons, it is important to find out which methodologies and tools are needed to construct or implement a solid data management strategy. By the way: *Which methodologies and tools are available to construct a master data management strategy?*

The research question can be subdivided into smaller units to ease understanding:

- What is master data? What is MDM?   What is a MDM strategy?
- How a master data management strategy has to be constructed?
- Which methodologies are available to construct a master data management strategy?
- Which tools are available to construct a master data management strategy?

1.3   Objective

It is crucial for companies to elaborate a master data management strategy and this has to be done in a way that is convenient, time and cost efficient. Restraining within boundaries set by the research question, this seminar thesis primarily aims at describing the available methodologies and tools facilitating the construction of a master data management strategy.

1.4   Structure of the paper

After presenting the problem statement, the research question and explaining the objective, this work goes forward with the definition of the core concepts, followed by the presentation of the methodologies used for the literature analysis and, finally the outputs of the conducted literature analysis.

2   Fundamentals and Basic terms

2.1   Master data

Master data refers to data repeatedly needed for the operations of a company and therefore must be saved permanently. This could be data related to customers and employees as well as suppliers, constituting one of the company's core components. Marco Spruit and Katharina Pietzka define master data as "data describing the most relevant business entities, on which the activities of an organization are based, e.g. counterparties, products or employees. In contrast to transactional data (invoices, orders, etc.) and inventory data, master data are oriented towards the attributes" Marco Spruit and Katharina Pietzka, "MD3M: The Master Data Management Maturity Model," *Computers in Human Behavior* 51 (2014): 1068–76

Andrew White et al. directly associate master data to a company's identity and define it as "the consistent and uniform set of identifiers and extended attributes that describe the core entities of the enterprise". Master data carry certain advantages in the management of business process, "analysis and communication across the enterprise", such as: their use involves "consistency, simplification and uniformity of process, analysis". For this reason, organizations apply for master data programs. As "a master data program helps organizations break down operational barriers, thus enabling greater enterprise agility and simplifying integration activities". Andrew White et al., "Mastering Master Data Management," *Gartner* 6, no. October (2014): 1–2.

To specify, what master data is. It is worth considering the opinions of some authors. According to Tyler Graham and Suzanne Selhorn, "the definition of "master" data varies by organization, but can be loosely defined as the nouns that describe all business processes. These nouns might be organisation-specific data, like your list of products or employees. They might be common reference data provided by external service [...] like address Information." TYLER GRAHAM and SUZANNE SELHORN, *Microsoft SQL Server 2008 R2 Master Data Services*, 2011.

Since, there is not a uniform definition of master data. Daniel Liebhart mentions Griffin [2005] in his book [SOA goes real]. Griffin presents a sample explanation, which can be considered as a general definition of the term master data: master data can be regarded as "information's that are necessary to create and support a company-wide system of central business entities as records". Daniel Liebhart, *SOA Goes Real: Service-Orientierte Architekturen Erfolgreich Planen Und Einführen* (Carl Hanser Verlag GmbH & Co. KG, 2007).

2.2 Master data management

The Management of master data is an important task in business operation. IBM defines it as "a set of disciplines, technologies and solutions that are used to create and maintain consistent, contextual and accurate business data for all stakeholders". In other words it is the "must have" toolbox for a company willing to better manage its resources and achieve success. IBM corporation, "Master Data Management : Looking beyond the Single View to Find the Right View .," no. April (2007).

Boris Otto and Andreas Reichert describe master data management as "an application-independent process" which helps organizations describing, owning and managing core business data entities. Thus, the management process of master data likely seems to be a Business Engineering (BE) task which requires organizational design. Boris Otto and Andreas Reichert, "Organizing Master Data Management: Findings from an Expert Survey," *Proceedings of the 2010 ACM Symposium on ...,* 2010, 106–10. Talking of Business Engineering, it acts as interface between knowledge in the field of business administration and information technology and sets it at the disposal of all transformation aspects ranging from presentation to process model and political consideration. Baumöl Ulrike and Jung Reinhard, "Wirtschaftsinformatik in Wissenschaft Und Praxis," in *Wirtschaftsinformatik in Wissenschaft Und Praxis*, 2014, 249–69.

Therefore, due to the different points of views, master data management as part of industrial data management is assigned to perform the following tasks:

- Description of master data strategy as well as the essential objectives and enterprise-wide policies and standards for the handling of master data, in the course of which the availability, integrity and security of master data is assured

- Pointing out the necessity of the acquisition administration and maintenance of master data

- Development of an information model for all master data objects at the enterprise level

- Development and maintenance of suitable master data architecture and if needed implementation of master data management and distribution systems

It possesses therefore a suitable element for organizational business management. Legner Christine and Boris Otto, "Stammdatenmanagement," no. July (2016).

2.3   Master data management strategy

The implementation of a sustainable master data management system is a big challenge faced by almost every company nowadays. It is even more challenging considering the fact that data quality measurement and monitoring has to be done on a continuous base. Precaution has to be taken to ensure a smooth process flow.

Allen Dreibelbis et al. define MDM Strategy as a "value-enabling combination of business and technical components. It needs to include the business participation, business motivation, and overall guidelines from the business". This is concerned by major issues, objectives, standards and guidelines, which the organization intends to achieve. Central part of this research work, a master data management strategy "addresses a wide variety of business and technical concerns within an enterprise. It is often wise to address these concerns incrementally. Incremental deployment allows significant value to be provided as each phase of an MDM project expands the capabilities of the MDM by integrating additional systems, extending the kinds of data managed, or providing new ways in which the master data may be used". Allen Dreibelbis et al., *Enterprise Master Data Management: An SOA Approach to Managing Core Information*, 2008.

Furthermore, defining a strategy to manage master data should always be highlighted because it constitutes the basis of successful MDM development in the enterprise. Companies with a well-defined master data management strategy are more advanced in their development than companies with none. The master data management strategy has to support the business strategy and take the IT strategy into account. This strategy also enables to define a business vison involving activity fields and reflecting wishes and priorities of decision makers. Henrik Packowski, Josef; Baumeier, Strategisches Stammdatenmanagement: Voraussetzung für agile und effiziente Geschäftsprozesse, 18–19, 48–49 (2012).

As mentioned by Martin Hubert Ofner et al., a strategy let decision maker specify directive of the MDM initiative. In other words, a strategy support them by specifying "important principles and guidelines which have an effect on the decisions". In this case, the main "goals of MDM initiative" should be defined based on the "business benefit". Thus, it is indispensable to clarify "which type of master data (typically customer, material, and supplier master data), which company units and departments, and which information systems (IS) are to be included". Martin Hubert Ofner et al., "Management of the Master Data Lifecycle: A Framework for Analysis," *Journal of Enterprise Information Management* 26, no. 4 (2013): 472–91.

3   Methodology for the literature work

3.1   Methodology

The process model of "Fettke" and „Webster & Watson" are taken in consideration to elaborate a literature review bringing an approach answering the research question of this seminar thesis.

The process model of "Fettke" describes how the literature review is done, as shown in the figure bellow.

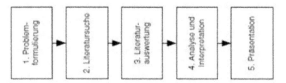

Figure 1: Process model for literature analysis according to Fettke

Moreover, the taxonomic classification of reviews according to Fettke has been used to develop a research design regrouping literature into special categories. This helps for example in shedding light on the focus of the research or to clearly identify the audience of the research work. See Table 2.

The "Webster & Watson model" has been used to conceptualize the topic based on relevance. This is done in the course of reading the different available papers. Afterwards, literature will be synthesized through discussion of overall ideas and consideration between the collected concepts. An example of the model is shown in the table 4-6.

3.2   Keywords and search queries

A list of keywords has been used to refine the literature research in order to cover all aspects and details of the topics. A popular search strategy basically consists in distinguishing between key-word and free text entries, whereby the final structure of a search word was often a combination of both.

- Synonyms have been considered during the selection of suitable search key words in order to increase the number of possible matches.

- Free text formulations are used to identify aspects that have not been covered using keywords indexing and hence identify shortcomings.

List of keywords: *master data, master data management, MDM strategy, "Stammdatenmanagement-Strategie", master data methodology, MDM strategy tools, corporate strategy, business strategy, Roadmap for master data management strategy.*

A systematic search in the database is performed with a combination of Tags. Each search entry is constructed in the following way: "Master data" AND "management", "Master data" AND "management" AND "strategy", "MDM strategy AND tool OR methodology, etc.

3.3   Search filter

Period of interest during research: 2007 – 2016, due to the large proliferation of multitouch smartphones and tablets computers as from the year 2007, there has been a leap in the business world thanks "mobile Internet". This of course automatically leads to an increased amount of master data. Customers and suppliers work on the go and this implies a large master data set. It therefore makes sense to consider a proper range.

Language of research: English and German, two languages are used to optimize the search result.

Keywords: they are used to refine the topic.

Abstract: abstract of books, articles and essays have been read to decide whether literature is worth considering or not.

3.4 Literature sources

The used literatures have been taken from following sources:

Journals/ databases	MDM	MDM + Strategy	MDM + solution	MDM+strategy+implementation/ development	MDM + strategy + construction	MDM+strategy+methodologies	MDM + strategy + tools	Business strategy + tools	Selected
ScienceDirect	5041	1696	2400	520	311	455	789	5522	6
ACM	42	0	9	0	0	0	0	2937	3
Emerald Insight	6	25	25	48	0	21	26	2396	4
IEEE	373	15	3	3	3	0	0	205	2
HBS	NA	NA	NA	NA	NA	NA	1	NA	1
IQH	NA	NA	NA	NA	NA	NA	1	NA	1
Google Scholar	1.320000	71100	72	150	3	10100	8380	14100 00	2
NCBI	NA	NA	NA	NA	NA	1	NA	NA	1
ResearchGate	NA	NA	NA	NA	NA	NA	1	1	2
Total Hits	Σ	Σ	Σ	Σ	Σ	Σ	Σ	Σ	**22**

Table 1: Search results of the structured analysis of journals and databases

Legend: IQH: International journal for Quality in Heath Care; NCBI: US national Center for biotechnology information; HBS: Haward business publishing

NA: Not applicable, because of the impossibility to fit the research to defined search principles (e.g.: period: 2007-2016)

3.5 Characterisation of literature analysis

Characteristic		Category			
1. Type		**Natural language**		Mathematical-statistical	
2. Focus		**Research findings**	Research method	Theory	Experience
3. Goal	Formulation	Implicit		**Explicit**	
	Content	**Integration**	Critical	Central issues	
4. Perspective		**Neutral**		Position	
5. Literature	Selection	Implicit		**Explicit**	
	Scope	key publications	representative	**selective**	complete
6. Structure		Historical	**Conceptual**	methodical	
7. Target group		Public	Practitioner	**General researcher**	**Specialized researcher**
8. Future research		Implicit		**Explicit**	

Table 2: Taxonomic classification according to Peter Fettke (2006)

4 Result of the Work

4.1 Construction of master data management strategy: methodologies and tools

4.1.1 Methodologies

A master data management strategy is aimed at elaborating a template defining a set of guidelines to be used during the implementation of a MDM system. This enables the detection of possible problems and insufficiency at early stages. The direct effect is a trouble-free implementation as long as the proposed strategy meets the necessary requirements. The master data manager should be able to identify and understand the risks that arise with strategy and also take counter measures to avoid them. To achieve that goal, it is meaningful to follow up every step involved in the strategy construction and consider the implications of each single step.

A clear strategy has a positive impact on the maturity level of master data management. This means, the MDM strategy defines the objectives and values of master data management. The strategy includes the "development of a vision, defining the MDM strategy, deriving an implementation plan, and setting the communication and change strategy". A MDM Strategy needs to be implemented to individual situations depending on the maturity level of the considered company. The following figure illustrates the relevant steps to be considered during the implementetion of a MDM strategy according to Baumeier and Packowski.

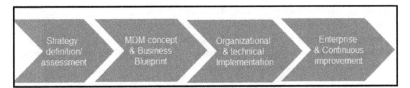

Figure 2: A methodology of a MDM Strategy construction inspired by Baumeier and Packowski [Source: Own illustration]

First of all, a strategy is assessed based on a clear vison and derived from business requirements. After that a MDM concept and business blueprint are established. This involves a concept elaboration and blueprint details for data models, processes and governance and IT architecture. Organizational and technical implementation is the next step. This refers to the realisation of defined concepts using available resources and MDM-technologies. Lastly, continuous operation and improvement have to be taken care of. This occurs by making use of feedbacks to conceive improvements initiatives. Packowski, Josef; Baumeier, Strategisches Stammdatenmanagement: Voraussetzung für agile und effiziente Geschäftsprozesse, 18–19, 48– 49 (2012).

For a successful planning during master data management, it is important to have an effective strategy. Hence, it makes sense to adopt a specific methodology. An example of such methodology has been developed by the corporate group "Collaborative". This is illustrated in the figure bellow.

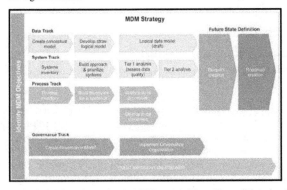

Figure 3: the six major tracks of a MDM strategy [Consulting collaborative, Page: 2 (2013)]]

The MDM Strategy starts by identifying Objectives. Key attributes are highlighted to determine "the needs of the business" which should be achieved. In the second step, the "data Track" consists in providing an "insight to determine what comprises the master data subject area in focus." The goal of the system track "is to gain an understanding of how master data is used, structured, and distributed in systems across the organization." Process track comprises of process inventory-related activities, the build of process list & approach, the capture of as-is process and lastly the development of to-be processes. The governance track "has two key areas: the development of a governance model for on- going data management and alignment of leadership and communications, including the building of a change management strategy." At the stage of future State definition, information gained throughout the project are consolidated and organized. The blueprint aims at providing a clear view of creative needs in business and technology solutions as well as data integrations. Consulting Collaborative, "Information Management: Master Data Management," *Master Data Management*, 2013, 1–2.

Further on master data management, it has to cover all relevant business domains such as customer, product, and employees and so on. Viswanathan presents a methodology based on tree horizons to construct a customer-oriented master data management strategy. This methodology shows a model performing a strategy program for customer data, i.e. customer data integration (CDI).

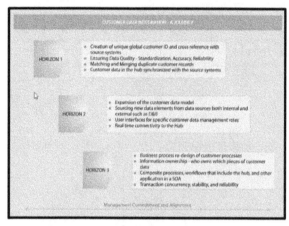

Figure 4: Steps building a MDM initiative focusing on customer perspective [Kalyan Viswanathan, page 7 (2007)]

Viswanathan justifies the effectiveness of focalizing on customer data by pointing out that "the CDI (Customer data integration) Market has gained momentum simply due the fact that in almost every business vertical, getting to know the customer is a critical business imperative. Customer data is also widely shared across numerous operational and analytical applications." The first horizon looks into providing a sort of reference that is unique to each customer. This reference comprises a unique global customer ID matching and merging duplicate customer records. Of course accuracy and reliability is verified and available data is synchronized with the source systems. The second phase involves expansion of the customer data model. This needs real time connectivity to the Hub as new data elements has to be sourced from both external and internal sources. The last horizon aims at redesigning the business process related to customer entities and establishing ownership right of customer information. Kalyan Viswanathan, "A Methodology for Sustainable Success with MDM Initiatives," 2007, 5–7.

Oracle uses five primary pillars as illustrated in the figure bellow to exemplify an implementation plan of MDM strategy.

Figure 5: Key pillars for MDM [Oracle; page 33 (2011)]

"Consolidation services manage the movement of master data into the central store". "Cleansing services deduplicate, standardize and augment the master data". "Governance services control access, retrieval, privacy, auditing, and change management rules". "Sharing services include integration, web services, ETL maps, event propagation, and global standards based synchronization". In case of customer data for example, the hub offers an enterprise a "comprehensive functionality" enabling "to manage customer data over the full customer lifecycle: capturing customer data, standardization and correction of names and addresses; identification and merging of duplicate records; enrichment of the customer profile; enforcement of compliance and risk policies; and the distribution of the "single source of truth" best version customer profile to operational systems". Oracle, "Master Data Management: An Oracle White Paper," *Master Data Management* 61 (2011): 33–35.

4.1.2   Evaluation of research findings: methodologies

As you can see in Table 4 (Appendix), it was not easy to find a clear methodology which can help to construct a master data management strategy. A lot of methodologies have been found but these don´t always fit together because the focus is based on the strategy. And each company has its own strategy and need therefore an adequate methodology to implement this strategy. Since each company has its own strategy, vision and philosophy, it is normal it makes sense when each organization has its specific methodology for strategy implementation.

4.1.3   Tools

After many researches on different databases and conferences, there wasn´t any research work directly presenting tools that help to build a MDM strategy. The most judicious alternative was to focus on tools used in setting business or corporate strategy.

The balance score card (BSC) is commonly used "as a tool to facilitate strategy implementation and demonstrate how to break down strategic goals into measurable elements". This approach leads to successful identifying of "key themes for strategy development, drafting a strategy map and developing strategic objectives and measures" The BSC is used in combination with "EFQM model to guide strategy development and implementation in health care organizations". Groene et al., "The Balanced Scorecard of Acute Settings: Development Process, Definition of 20 Strategic Objectives and Implementation," *International Journal for Quality in Health Care,*

2009. Referring to EFQM Model (European Foundation for Quality Management), it is a "model using Fuzzy Logic, Analytical Hierarchy Process (AHP) technique and Operations Research (OR) model to improve the organizations' excellence level by increasing the quality of business performance evaluation and determining of improvement projects with high priority" The model has been developed in 1998. It provides an enterprise an "executive tool" that supports them "to measure how much they are in the path of organizational excellence and evaluate their balanced growth". Jamal Hosseini Ezzabadi, Mohammad Dehghani Saryazdi, and Ali Mostafaeipour, "Implementing Fuzzy Logic and AHP into the EFQM Model for Performance Improvement: A Case Study," *Applied Soft Computing* 36 (2015): 165–76.

The Balanced Scorecard enables business managers to establish mission and Vision Statements into a comprehensive set of objectives and performance measures that can be quantified and evaluated.

Focusing on the organizational level, Robert S. Kaplan and David Norton tried to construct a management system using a BSC as "management strategic system". This was inspired by the fact that BSC comprises strategy vision, financial, customer, internal business process perspectives involving performance measures. The main objective is to construct a data management strategy translating business vision and strategy. The BSC has been "initially conceived as an organizational performance measurement tool that included non-financial as well as financial measures. By ensuring that all of the objectives and measures inherent to it are derived from an organization's vision and its resulting strategy, Strategy-Focused Organizations have transformed the Balanced Scorecard from a performance management tool into a strategic tool". Robert S. Kaplan and David P. Norton, "The Strategy- Focused Organization," *Harvard Business School Press* 23, no. 1 (2001): 1–8.

A study about the use of the BSC approach in ERP implementation presents a balance scorecard as "a systematic approach to ERP performance measurement". In this context, the BSC "offers a methodology to assess the performance of different ERP implementations" and help to align "ERP implementation and operation with strategic objectives through a series of quantifiable performance measurement indicators". Enterprises using ERP systems resort to BSC in order to align its implementation and its operation with strategic objectives from a several performance measurement indicators. Yung-Chi Shen, Pih-Shuw Chen, and Chun-Hsien Wang, "A Study of Enterprise Resource Planning (ERP) System Performance Measurement Using the Quantitative Balanced Scorecard Approach," *Computers in Industry* 75 (2016): 127–39.

Nevertheless, the BSC pioneers create another tool called "strategy map". A strategy map "addresses the human capital needs of the new strategy in objective. The details of these requirements will be described in lower-level human resources plans". It "provided a framework to align its human capital, information capital, and organization readiness to the strategy with sufficient specific detail to be meaningful, measurable, and actionable". "The strategy map describes the logic of the strategy, clearly showing the objectives for the critical internal processes that create value and the intangible assets required to support them".

Moreover, the main goals of a strategy map are: description strategy logic and clearly presentation of objectives for the critical internal processes. Strategy maps are popular by organizations and have been recognized as a powerful tool enabling to depict and formulate strategy. The framework helps therefore to construct a well-understood strategy across the company. Sheila Corrall, "Capturing the Contribution of Subject Librarians: Applying Strategy

Maps and Balanced Scorecards to Liaison Work," *Library Management* 36, no. 3 (2015): 223–34.

Guoliang Yang et al present the use of strategy maps in the real life with an example of NRIs based on customer view. NRI is the national research institute. NRIs had to meet objectives which facilitate the governance by creating "long-term values for the country and society" An illustration to how the model is integrated is presented in the figure bellow. NRISs challenge is to provide a strategy including fundamental researches integrated systems, and high-tech-innovations, referring to adequate development. Guoliang Yang et al., "Developing Performance Measures and Setting Their Targets for National Research Institutes Based on Strategy Maps," *Journal of Science and Technology Policy Management* 6, no. 2 (2015): 165–86.

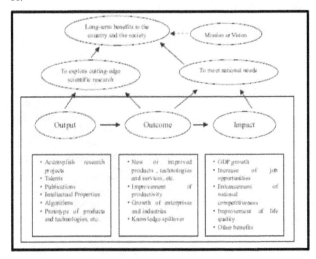

Figure 6: NRIs' strategy map from the client perspective [Guoliang Yang et al, page: 172 (2015)]

Always talking about MDM strategy, Knowledgent has published in 2014 a white paper pointing the importance of considering MDM architecture when constructing a MDM strategy because enterprise application architecture facilitate the availability of master data across all business areas. To ensure high quality in master data processing, the architecture "should include critical capabilities, such as master/reference data source identification, master data acquisition, metadata master hub management, integration, and access" This reference architecture has two hub areas. The first area concerns metadata management and is composed of following functions: "Hub data modelling", "Rules Management", "User management", "security and Access", and "Performance and scalability". The second layer is aimed at providing support to the master data management itself. Here, the data are primarily uploaded from several sources, and then they are standardized and cleaned to ensure proper data validation. The process continues with "match and merge" stage which enables automatic or manual merging of master into a record. The next step is about the hierarchy management. It "provides the ability to manage relationship structures across master data records with the goal of viewing those records in a hierarchical presentation (e.g., customers by territory, vertical, size)". The last stage refers to "Stewardship and Reporting" which provides easy-to-use-interfaces enabling to have access to rules, reporting and data management functions. Knowledgent, "Developing an MDM Strategy: Key Components for Success Table of Contents," *Knowledgent White Paper Series* 10 (2014).

4.1.4   Evaluation of research findings: tools

Talking about sustainable strategy is always the best thing, organizations think about. But it would be even better to talk about tools enabling to construct a master data management strategy. That is one of big challenges of organizations nowadays. Since, it is very difficult to have a tool helping to construct a MDM strategy, alternative have been adopted. Most companies make use of business strategy tools to support their MDM strategy implementation. See illustration in Table 5(Appendix).

5   Discussion and conclusion

5.1   Discussion

After a thorough literature analysis, this research found several concepts (methodologies in this case) proposed by different authors. As illustrated in the table 4, there are not many literatures about methodologies used in master data construction strategy. Some authors like Pakowski and Baumeier present the relevance of defining a methodology enabling the construction of a MDM strategy and point out the importance of blueprint when developing a MDM strategy.

A blueprint supports organizations on planning and managing its several business initiatives. It offers them a model clearly presenting several tasks, stages and all activities that are comprised in the current management approach. Elizabeth Mcleod et al., "A Blueprint for Blue Carbon: Toward an Improved Understanding of the Role of Vegetated Coastal Habitats in Sequestering CO_2," *The Ecology Society of America* 9, no. 10 (2011).

Due to the lack of literature references in case of tools enabling the construction of a MDM strategy, the research has been oriented to tools used in business strategy elaboration. The research result presents two main MDM strategy creation tools. The first tool is a BSC system and the second is the strategic map, which is a derived tool of the BSC.

Trying to establish a concept matrix added with unit of Analysis according to Webster and Watson (See Table 6 in Appendix), with methodologies as unit of analysis, this led to no results. This is because there were no standard methodologies and/tools available to construct a MDM Strategy.

As reported in previous analysed literatures, the favourable solution for the construction of a MDM strategy is the adoption of business strategy tools like BSC or strategy maps. Each company can hence develop its own implementation methodology meeting its needs and requirements.

As each research study, this research work had limitations. The main focus of this study was to find available methodologies and tools which can help organizations to construct a strategy making easier the management of master data. Since there was no founded tool fit together with any methodology, the conclusion was to take business strategy tools into account to support enterprises on MDM implementation.

Further researches need to be done conducting "empirical research" to verify why it is so difficult to have tools enabling to construct a master data management strategy. Researchers can try for example to discuss with business Enabler concerning their used application for the implementation of master data management strategy. However, this should be done with strictest anonymity of involved companies.

5.2   Conclusion

Strategy is very important for each company dealing with master data. Having tools and methodologies to construct it, still represents a serious challenge for organizations. The current survey showed that a comprehensive master management strategy is crucial to company success. This enables enterprises to know where to start, how to execute this strategy and how this can be profitable for the whole company.

Literature

Christine, Legner, and Boris Otto. "Stammdatenmanagement," no. July (2016).

Collaborative, Consulting. "Information Management: Master Data Management." *Master Data Management*, 2013, 1–2.

Corall, Sheila. "Capturing the Contribution of Subject Librarians: Applying Strategy Maps and Balanced Scorecards to Liaison Work." *Library Management* 36, no. 3 (2015): 223–34. doi:doi:10.1108/LM-09-2014-0101.

Dreibelbis, Allen, Eberhard Hechler, Ivan Milman, Martin Oberhofer, Paul Van Run, and Dan Wolfson. *Enterprise Master Data Management: An SOA Approach to Managing Core Information*, 2008.

GRAHAM, TYLER, and SUZANNE SELHORN. *Microsoft SQL Server 2008 R2 Master Data Services*, 2011.

Groene, Brandt E, Schmidt W, and Moeller J. "The Balanced Scorecard of Acute Settings: Development Process, Definition of 20 Strategic Objectives and Implementation." *International Journal for Quality in Health Care*, 2009. doi:10.1093/intqhc/mzp024.

Hosseini Ezzabadi, Jamal, Mohammad Dehghani Saryazdi, and Ali Mostafaeipour. "Implementing Fuzzy Logic and AHP into the EFQM Model for Performance Improvement: A Case Study." *Applied Soft Computing* 36 (2015): 165–76. http://www.sciencedirect.com/science/article/pii/S1568494615004287.

Hubert Ofner, Martin, Kevin Straub, Boris Otto, and Hubert Oesterle. "Management of the Master Data Lifecycle: A Framework for Analysis." *Journal of Enterprise Information Management* 26, no. 4 (2013): 472–91. doi:10.1108/JEIM-05-2013-0026.

IBM corporation. "Master Data Management : Looking beyond the Single View to Find the Right View .," no. April (2007).

Kaplan, Robert S., and David P. Norton. "The Strategy- Focused Organization." *Harvard Business School Press* 23, no. 1 (2001): 1–8. doi:10.5465/AMLE.2005.19086796.

Knowledgent. "Developing an MDM Strategy: Key Components for Success Table of Contents." *Knowledgent White Paper Series* 10 (2014).

Liebhart, Daniel. *SOA Goes Real: Service-Orientierte Architekturen Erfolgreich Planen Und Einführen.* Carl Hanser Verlag GmbH & Co. KG, 2007.

Mcleod, Elizabeth, Gail L. Chmura, Steven Bouillon, Rodney Salm, Mats Björk, Carlos M Duarte, Catherine E Lovelock, William H Schlesinger, and Brian R Silliam. "A Blueprint for Blue Carbon: Toward an Improved Understanding of the Role of Vegetated Coastal Habitats in Sequestering $CO2$." *The Ecology Society of America* 9, no. 10 (2011): 552–60. doi:10.1890/110004.

Oracle. "Master Data Management: An Oracle White Paper." *Master Data Management* 61 (2011): 33–35.

Otto, Boris, and Andreas Reichert. "Organizing Master Data Management: Findings from an Expert Survey." *Proceedings of the 2010 ACM Symposium on ...*, 2010, 106–10. doi:10.1145/1774088.1774111.

Packowski, Josef; Baumeier, Henrik. Strategisches Stammdatenmanagement: Voraussetzung für agile und effiziente Geschäftsprozesse, 18–19, 48–49, (2012).

Shen, Yung-Chi, Pih-Shuw Chen, and Chun-Hsien Wang. "A Study of Enterprise Resource Planning (ERP) System Performance Measurement Using the Quantitative Balanced Scorecard Approach." *Computers in Industry* 75 (2016): 127–39.

doi:10.1016/j.compind.2015.05.006.

Spruit, Marco, and Katharina Pietzka. "MD3M: The Master Data Management Maturity Model." *Computers in Human Behavior* 51 (2014): 1068–76. http://dx.doi.org/10.1016/j.chb.2014.09.030.

Ulrike, Baumöl, and Jung Reinhard. "Wirtschaftsinformatik in Wissenschaft Und Praxis." In *Wirtschaftsinformatik in Wissenschaft Und Praxis*, 249–69, 2014. doi:10.1007/978-3-642-54411-8.

Viswanathan, Kalyan. "A Methodology for Sustainable Success with MDM Initiatives," 2007, 5–7.

White, Andrew, David Newman, Debra Logan, and John Radcliffe. "Mastering Master Data Management." *Gartner* 6, no. October (2014): 1–2.

Yang, Guoliang, Alasdair Macnab, Liying Yang, and Chunliang Fan. "Developing Performance Measures and Setting Their Targets for National Research Institutes Based on Strategy Maps." *Journal of Science and Technology Policy Management* 6, no. 2 (2015): 165–86. doi:10.1108/JSTPM-12-2014-0042.

Appendix

ID	Articles	Authors
1	MD3M: The Master Data Management Maturity Model	**M. Spruit and K. Pietzka**
2	Mastering Master Data Management	**Andrew White, David Newman, Debra Logan, John Radcliffe**
3	Master Data Management : Looking beyond the Single View to Find the Right View	**IBM corporation**
4	Organizing Master Data Management: Findings from an Expert Survey	**Boris Otto and Andreas Reichert**
5	Stammdatenmanagement	**Legner Christine and Boris Otto**
6	Strategisches Stammdatenmanagement: Voraussetzung für agile und effiziente Geschäftsprozesse	**Packowski, Josef; Baumeier, Henrik**
7	Management of the Master Data Lifecycle: A Framework for Analysis	**Martin Hubert Ofner et al.**
8	Information Management: Master Data Management	**Collaborative Consulting**
9	A Methodology for Sustainable Success with MDM Initiatives	**Viswanathan, Kalyan**
10	Master Data Management: An Oracle white paper	**Oracle corporation**
11	The Balanced Scorecard of acute settings: development process, definition of 20 strategic objectives and implementation	**Groene et al.**
12	Implementing Fuzzy Logic and AHP into the EFQM model for performance improvement: A case study	**Hosseini et al.**
13	The Strategy- Focused Organization	**Robert Kaplan and David Norton**
14	A study of enterprise resource planning (ERP) system performance measurement using the quantitative balanced scorecard approach	**Y. Shen, P. Chen and C. Wang**
15	Capturing the contribution of subject librarians: Applying strategy maps and balanced scorecards to liaison work	**Corall, Sheila**
16	Developing performance measures and setting their targets for national research institutes based on strategy maps	**G. Yang, A. Macnab, L. Yang et al.**
17	Developing an MDM Strategy: Key Components for Success Table of Contents	**Knowledgent**

Table 3: List of analyzed literatures

ID	Methodologies (e.g.: A = Methodology A)			
	A	B	C	D
1	X	0	0	0
2	0	0	X	0
3	0	0	0	0
4	0	0	X	0
5	XX	0	0	0
6	XXX	0	0	0
7	XX	0	X	X
8	0	XXX	0	0
9	0	0	XXX	0
10	0	0	0	XXX
11	0	0	0	0
12	0	0	0	0
13	0	0	0	0
14	0	0	0	0
15	0	0	0	0
16	0	0	0	0
17	X	0	0	0

Legend: X (abstract), XX (detailed), XXX (well-detailed); Methodology A: See Figure 2; Methodology B: See Figure 3; Methodology C: See Figure 4; Methodology D: See Figure 5

Table 4: concept matrix about methodologies for MDM Strategy referring to analyzed literatures (Inspired by Webster and Watson)

ID	Tools	
	Tool 1	Tool 2
1	0	0
2	0	0
3	0	0
4	0	0
5	X	0
6	0	0
7	0	0
8	0	0
9	0	0
10	0	0
11	X	X
12	X	0
13	X	X
14	X	0
15	X	X
16	X	X
17	0	0
Legend: Tool 1: Balance scorecard, Tool 2: Strategy maps		

Table 5: Concept matrix about business strategy tools referring to analyzed literatures (inspired by Webster and Watson)

Articles(ID)	Tools							
	Tool 1				Tool 2			
Methodologies	A	B	C	D	A	B	C	D
1	0	0	0	0	0	0	0	0
2	0	0	0	0	0	0	0	0
3	0	0	0	0	0	0	0	0
4	0	0	0	0	0	0	0	0
5	0	0	0	0	0	0	0	0
6	0	0	0	0	0	0	0	0
7	0	0	0	0	0	0	0	0
8	0	0	0	0	0	0	0	0
9	0	0	0	0	0	0	0	0
10	0	0	0	0	0	0	0	0
11	0	0	0	0	0	0	0	0
12	0	0	0	0	0	00	0	0
13	0	0	0	0	0	0	0	0
14	0	0	0	0	0	0	0	0
15	0	0	0	0	0	0	0	0
16	0	0	0	0	0	0	0	0
17	0	0	0	0	0	0	0	0

Table 6: concept matrix augmented with unit of Analysis according to Webster and Watson

www.ingramcontent.com/pod-product-compliance
Lightning Source LLC
LaVergne TN
LVHW042314060326
832902LV00009B/1476